GIFT FROM THE SEA

Anne Morrow Lindbergh

GIFT FROM THE SEA

Introduction by Reeve Lindbergh

PANTHEON BOOKS, NEW YORK

The quotation from Auden on page 64 is reprinted courtesy of
Random House, Inc. The afterword, "*Gift from the Sea* Re-opened,"
was written to accompany an article on *Gift from the Sea* published
by *McCall's* magazine in their August 1975 issue.

Library of Congress Cataloging-in-Publication Data
Lindbergh, Anne Morrow, 1906–2001
Gift from the Sea
1. Life.   I. Title.
BD435.L52 1977 170'.202'233 76-56244
ISBN 0-679-40683-2
Special Markets ISBN: 978-0-5256-1557-6

Book design by Fearn Cutler
Cover design by Jenny Carrow

Printed in the United States of America
4th Printing

Contents

Introduction to the
Fiftieth Anniversary Edition

My mother published this book over fifty years ago, and I feel as if I have read it fifty times since then. I may not be exaggerating. Gift from the Sea first came out when I was ten years old, and this edition is appearing in my sixtieth year. I blush to confess that I'd never read the book at all until I was in my twenties, though this is not uncommon for the children of writers, whoever they may be. Now I read it at least once a year, sometimes twice or more.

I read Gift from the Sea at all seasons of the year and of

Introduction

my life. I have never once had the sense that my mother's 1955 book has lost its freshness, or that the wisdom contained within its pages has ceased to apply, whether to my own life or to what I have learned, over time, of hers.

When my mother was writing the book, she stayed in a little cottage near the beach on Captiva Island, on Florida's Gulf Coast. Many people have claimed to know which cottage it was and where it stands today, but the Florida friends who originally found the place for her told me years ago that the cottage had been gone, even then, for a long time.

Knowing this to be true, I went to spend a week on Captiva recently, bringing with me the copy of Gift from the Sea that my mother had inscribed in 1955, quite simply, "for Reeve." It was not the writer's cottage that I was looking for on the shores of the Gulf of Mexico, but the writer.

Following her death and the subsequent estate processes, following several celebrations and events related to our public family history, and following a number of revelations and discussions about our personal family history, I was looking to her, again, for help. I felt that I needed her wisdom and her encouragement, one more time, to carry me forward. Just as I had hoped and expected, she did not fail me.

Introduction

At whatever point one opens Gift from the Sea, to any chapter or page, the author's words offer a chance to breathe and to live more slowly. The book makes it possible to quiet down and rest in the present, no matter what the circumstances may be. Just to read it—a little of it or in its entirety—is to exist for a while in a different and more peaceful tempo.

Even the sway and flow of language and cadence seem to me to make reference to the easy, inevitable movements of the sea. I don't know whether my mother wrote this way consciously, or whether it came as a natural result of living on the beach, day after day, while writing the book. Whatever the reason, after just a few pages I always begin to relax into that movement and to feel like something that belongs to the tide—just another piece of flotsam floating in the great oceanic rhythms of the universe. This, in itself, is deeply reassuring.

But there is more than peace offered in this book, and more than the comforting tidal rhythms of quiet living and quiet words. Underlying all of it is an enormous, sustaining strength. It surprises me every time I meet this strength again in full force in Gift from the Sea. I tend to forget this quality in my mother, or maybe I've just taken it for granted.

I remember how small and delicate she always seemed. I remem-

Introduction

her her intelligence and her sensitivity. But when I reread Gift from the Sea, the illusion of fragility falls away, leaving the truth. How could I forget? She was, after all, a woman who raised five children after tragically losing her first son in 1932. She was the first woman in America to earn a first-class glider pilot's license, in 1930, and the first woman ever to win the National Geographic Society's Hubbard Medal, in 1934, for her aviation and exploration adventures. She also received the National Book Award, in 1938, for Listen! The Wind, her novel based on those adventures, and she remained a best-selling author all her life.

She skied with me in Vermont when she was sixty-five and took long walks in the Swiss Alps at seventy. Five years later, at seventy-five, she hiked down into Haleakala Crater in Maui, Hawaii, to spend a night in the volcano with several of her children and her friends.

I remember looking up in darkness at the great curved bowl of the night sky, bright with stars, while my mother, standing firm in her size-five hiking boots, pointed out and identified for us the Navigator's Circle—Cappella, Castor, Pollux, Procyon, and Sirius. They were the stars by which she had first learned to set a course in the darkness as a pioneer aviator fifty years earlier.

Introduction

. . .

Above all, I think, Gift from the Sea *offers its readers an unusual kind of freedom. It is hard to recognize, or even to describe, but I think this freedom is the real reason the book continues to be so well loved and so well read after all these years. I am talking about the freedom that comes from choosing to remain open, as my mother did, to life itself, whatever it may bring: joys, sorrows, triumphs, failures, suffering, comfort, and certainly, always, change.*

In honest reflection upon her own experience, in trying to live from a core of inner stillness while actively responding, as we all must do, to the "here and the now," my mother quietly set herself free, into her own life and into all life. By writing Gift from the Sea, *she found a new way to live in the world, for herself and for others. It is a joy to know that with this fiftieth anniversary edition a whole new generation of readers will be able to follow her.*

Reeve Lindbergh
St. Johnsbury, Vermont
March 2005

GIFT FROM THE SEA

I began these pages for myself, in order to think out my own particular pattern of living, my own individual balance of life, work and human relationships. And since I think best with a pencil in my hand, I started naturally to write. I had the feeling, when the thoughts first clarified on paper, that my experience was very different from other people's. (Are we all under this illusion?) My situation had, in certain ways, more freedom than that of most people, and in certain other ways, much less.

Gift from the Sea

Besides, I thought, not all women are searching for a new pattern of living, or want a contemplative corner of their own. Many women are content with their lives as they are. They manage amazingly well, far better than I, it seemed to me, looking at their lives from the outside. With envy and admiration, I observed the porcelain perfection of their smoothly ticking days. Perhaps they had no problems, or had found the answers long ago. No, I decided, these discussions would have value and interest only for myself.

But as I went on writing and simultaneously talking with other women, young and old, with different lives and experiences—those who supported themselves, those who wished careers, those who were hard-working housewives and mothers, and those with more ease—I found that my point of view was not unique. In varying settings and under different forms, I discovered that many women, and men too, were grappling with essentially the same questions as I, and were hungry to discuss and argue and hammer out possible answers. Even those whose lives had appeared to be ticking imperturbably under their smiling clock-faces were often trying, like me, to evolve another rhythm with more creative pauses in it, more adjustment to their individual needs, and new and more alive relationships to themselves as well as others.

Gift from the Sea

And so gradually, these chapters, fed by conversations, arguments and revelations from men and women of all groups, became more than my individual story, until I decided in the end to give them back to the people who had shared and stimulated many of these thoughts. Here, then, with my warm feelings of gratitude and companionship for those working along the same lines, I return my gift from the sea.

· 1 ·

THE BEACH

The beach is not the place to work; to read, write or think. I should have remembered that from other years. Too warm, too damp, too soft for any real mental discipline or sharp flights of spirit. One never learns. Hopefully, one carries down the faded straw bag, lumpy with books, clean paper, long over-due unanswered letters, freshly sharpened pencils, lists and good intentions. The books remain unread, the pencils break their points and the pads rest smooth and unblemished as the cloudless sky. No reading, no writing, no thoughts even—at least, not at first.

At first, the tired body takes over completely. As on shipboard, one descends into a deck-chair apathy. One is forced against one's mind, against all tidy resolutions, back into the primeval rhythms of the seashore. Rollers on the beach, wind in the pines, the slow flapping of herons across sand dunes, drown out the hectic rhythms of city and suburb, time tables and schedules. One falls under their spell, relaxes, stretches out prone. One becomes, in fact, like the element on which one lies, flattened by the sea; bare, open, empty as the beach, erased by today's tides of all yesterday's scribblings.

And then, some morning in the second week, the mind wakes, comes to life again. Not in a city sense —no—but beach-wise. It begins to drift, to play, to turn over in gentle careless rolls like those lazy waves on the beach. One never knows what chance treasures these easy unconscious rollers may toss up, on the smooth white sand of the conscious mind; what perfectly rounded stone, what rare shell from the ocean floor. Perhaps a channelled whelk, a moon shell or even an argonaut.

But it must not be sought for or—heaven forbid! —dug for. No, no dredging of the sea bottom here. That would defeat one's purpose. The sea does not reward those who are too anxious, too greedy, or too impatient. To dig for treasures shows not only impatience and greed, but lack of faith. Patience, patience, patience, is what the sea teaches. Patience and faith. One should lie empty, open, choiceless as a beach— waiting for a gift from the sea.

· 2 ·

CHANNELLED WHELK

The shell in my hand is deserted. It once housed a whelk, a snail-like creature, and then temporarily, after the death of the first occupant, a little hermit crab, who has run away, leaving his tracks behind him like a delicate vine on the sand. He ran away, and left me his shell. It was once a protection to him. I turn the shell in my hand, gazing into the wide open door from which he made his exit. Had it become an encumbrance? Why did he run away? Did he hope to find a better home, a better mode of living? I too have run away, I realize, I have shed the shell of my life, for these few weeks of vacation.

But his shell—it is simple; it is bare, it is beautiful. Small, only the size of my thumb, its architecture is perfect, down to the finest detail. Its shape, swelling like a pear in the center, winds in a gentle spiral to the pointed apex. Its color, dull gold, is whitened by a wash of salt from the sea. Each whorl, each faint knob, each criss-cross vein in its egg-shell texture, is as clearly defined as on the day of creation. My eye follows with delight the outer circumference of that diminutive winding staircase up which this tenant used to travel.

My shell is not like this, I think. How untidy it has become! Blurred with moss, knobby with barnacles, its shape is hardly recognizable any more. Surely, it had a shape once. It has a shape still in my mind. What is the shape of my life?

The shape of my life today starts with a family. I have a husband, five children and a home just beyond

Channelled Whelk

the suburbs of New York. I have also a craft, writing, and therefore work I want to pursue. The shape of my life is, of course, determined by many other things; my background and childhood, my mind and its education, my conscience and its pressures, my heart and its desires. I want to give and take from my children and husband, to share with friends and community, to carry out my obligations to man and to the world, as a woman, as an artist, as a citizen.

But I want first of all—in fact, as an end to these other desires—to be at peace with myself. I want a singleness of eye, a purity of intention, a central core to my life that will enable me to carry out these obligations and activities as well as I can. I want, in fact— to borrow from the language of the saints—to live "in grace" as much of the time as possible. I am not using this term in a strictly theological sense. By grace I mean an inner harmony, essentially spiritual, which can be translated into outward harmony. I am seeking perhaps what Socrates asked for in the prayer from the *Phaedrus* when he said, "May the outward and inward man be at one." I would like to achieve a state of inner spiritual grace from which I could function and give as I was meant to in the eye of God.

Vague as this definition may be, I believe most people are aware of periods in their lives when they seem to be "in grace" and other periods when they feel "out of grace," even though they may use different words to describe these states. In the first happy condition, one seems to carry all one's tasks before one lightly, as if borne along on a great tide; and in the opposite state one can hardly tie a shoe-string. It is true that a large part of life consists in learning a technique of tying the shoe-string, whether one is in grace or not. But there are techniques of living too; there are even techniques in the search for grace. And techniques can be cultivated. I have learned by some experience, by many examples and by the writings of countless others before me, also occupied in the search, that certain environments, certain modes of life, certain rules of conduct are more conducive to inner and outer harmony than others. There are, in fact, certain roads that one may follow. Simplification of life is one of them.

Channelled Whelk

I mean to lead a simple life, to choose a simple shell I can carry easily—like a hermit crab. But I do not. I find that my frame of life does not foster simplicity. My husband and five children must make their way in the world. The life I have chosen as wife and mother entrains a whole caravan of complications. It involves a house in the suburbs and either household drudgery or household help which wavers between scarcity and non-existence for most of us. It involves food and shelter; meals, planning, marketing, bills and making the ends meet in a thousand ways. It involves not only the butcher, the baker, the candlestickmaker but countless other experts to keep my modern house with its modern "simplifications" (electricity, plumbing, refrigerator, gas-stove, oil-burner, dish-washer, radios, car and numerous other labor-saving devices) functioning properly. It involves health; doctors, dentists, appointments, medicine, cod-liver oil, vitamins, trips to the drugstore. It involves education, spiritual, intellectual, physical; schools, school conferences, car-pools, extra trips for basketball or orchestra practice; tutoring; camps, camp equipment and transportation. It involves clothes, shopping, laundry, cleaning, mending, letting skirts down and sewing buttons on, or finding someone else to do it. It involves friends, my husband's, my children's, my own, and endless arrangements to get together; letters, invitations, telephone calls and transportation hither and yon.

For life today in America is based on the premise of ever-widening circles of contact and communication. It involves not only family demands, but community demands, national demands, international demands on the good citizen, through social and cultural pressures, through newspapers, magazines, radio programs, political drives, charitable appeals and so on. My mind reels with it. What a circus act we women perform every day of our lives. It puts the trapeze artist to shame. Look at us. We run a tight rope daily, balancing a pile of books on the head. Baby-carriage, parasol, kitchen chair, still under control. Steady now!

This is not the life of simplicity but the life of multiplicity that the wise men warn us of. It leads not to unification but to fragmentation. It does not bring grace; it destroys the soul. And this is not only true of

Channelled Whelk

my life, I am forced to conclude; it is the life of millions of women in America. I stress America, because today, the American woman more than any other has the privilege of choosing such a life. Woman in large parts of the civilized world has been forced back by war, by poverty, by collapse, by the sheer struggle to survive, into a smaller circle of immediate time and space, immediate family life, immediate problems of existence. The American woman is still relatively free to choose the wider life. How long she will hold this enviable and precarious position no one knows. But her particular situation has a significance far above its apparent economic, national or even sex limitations.

For the problem of the multiplicity of life not only confronts the American woman, but also the American man. And it is not merely the concern of the American as such, but of our whole modern civilization, since life in America today is held up as the ideal of a large part of the rest of the world. And finally, it is not limited to our present civilization, though we are faced with it now in an exaggerated form. It has always been one of the pitfalls of mankind.

Gift from the Sea

Plotinus was preaching the dangers of multiplicity of the world back in the third century. Yet, the problem is particularly and essentially woman's. Distraction is, always has been, and probably always will be, inherent in woman's life.

For to be a woman is to have interests and duties, raying out in all directions from the central mother-core, like spokes from the hub of a wheel. The pattern of our lives is essentially circular. We must be open to all points of the compass; husband, children, friends, home, community; stretched out, exposed, sensitive like a spider's web to each breeze that blows, to each call that comes. How difficult for us, then, to achieve a balance in the midst of these contradictory tensions, and yet how necessary for the proper functioning of our lives. How much we need, and how arduous of attainment is that steadiness preached in all rules for holy living. How desirable and how distant is the ideal of the contemplative, artist or saint—the inner inviolable core, the single eye.

With a new awareness, both painful and humorous, I begin to understand why the saints were rarely married women. I am convinced it has nothing inherently to do, as I once supposed, with chastity or children. It has to do primarily with distractions. The bearing, rearing, feeding and educating of children; the running of a house with its thousand details; human relationships with their myriad pulls—woman's normal occupations in general run counter to creative life, or contemplative life, or saintly life. The problem is not merely one of *Woman and Career, Woman and the Home, Woman and Independence.* It is more basically: how to remain whole in the midst of the distractions of life; how to remain balanced, no matter what centrifugal forces tend to pull one off center; how to remain strong, no matter what shocks come in at the periphery and tend to crack the hub of the wheel.

What is the answer? There is no easy answer, no complete answer. I have only clues, shells from the sea. The bare beauty of the channelled whelk tells me that one answer, and perhaps a first step, is in simplification of life, in cutting out some of the distractions. But how? Total retirement is not possible. I cannot shed my responsibilities. I cannot permanently inhabit a desert island. I cannot be a nun in the midst of family life. I would not want to be. The solution for me, surely, is neither in total renunciation of the world, nor in total acceptance of it. I must find a balance somewhere, or an alternating rhythm between these two extremes; a swinging of the pendulum between solitude and communion, between retreat and return. In my periods of retreat, perhaps I can learn something to carry back into my worldly life. I can at least practice for these two weeks the simplification of outward life, as a beginning. I can follow this superficial clue, and see where it leads. Here, in beach living, I can try.

· · ·

One learns first of all in beach living the art of shedding; how little one can get along with, not how much. Physical shedding to begin with, which then mysteriously spreads into other fields. Clothes, first. Of course, one needs less in the sun. But one needs less anyway, one finds suddenly. One does not need a closet-full, only a small suitcase-full. And what a relief it is! Less taking up and down of hems, less mending and—best of all—less worry about what to wear. One finds one is shedding not only clothes— but vanity.

Next, shelter. One does not need the airtight shelter one has in winter in the North. Here I live in a bare sea-shell of a cottage. No heat, no telephone, no plumbing to speak of, no hot water, a two-burner oil stove, no gadgets to go wrong. No rugs. There were some, but I rolled them up the first day; it is easier to sweep the sand off a bare floor. But I find I don't bustle about with unnecessary sweeping and cleaning here. I am no longer aware of the dust. I have shed my Puritan conscience about absolute tidiness and cleanliness. Is it possible that, too, is a material burden? No curtains. I do not need them for privacy; the pines around my house are enough protection. I want the windows open all the time, and I don't want to worry about rain. I begin to shed my Martha-like anxiety about many things. Washable slipcovers, faded and old—I hardly see them; I don't worry about the impression they make on other people. I am shedding pride. As little furniture as possible; I shall not need much. I shall ask into my shell only those friends with whom I can be completely honest. I find I am shedding hypocrisy in human relationships. What a rest that will be! The most exhausting thing in life, I have discovered, is being insincere. That is why so much of social life is exhausting; one is wearing a mask. I have shed my mask.

I find I live quite happily without those things I think necessary in winter in the North. And as I write these words, I remember, with some shock at the disparity in our lives, a similar statement made by a friend of mine in France who spent three years in a German prison camp. Of course, he said, qualifying his remark, they did not get enough to eat, they were sometimes atrociously treated, they had little physical freedom. And yet, prison life taught him how little one can get along with, and what extraordinary spiritual freedom and peace such simplification can bring. I remember again, ironically, that today more of us in America than anywhere else in the world have the luxury of choice between simplicity and complication of life. And for the most part, we, who could choose simplicity, choose complication. War, prison, survival periods, enforce a form of simplicity on man. The monk and the nun choose it of their own free will. But if one accidentally finds it, as I have for a few days, one finds also the serenity it brings.

Is it not rather ugly, one may ask? One collects material possessions not only for security, comfort or vanity, but for beauty as well. Is your sea-shell house not ugly and bare? No, it is beautiful, my house. It is bare, of course, but the wind, the sun, the smell of the pines blow through its bareness. The unfinished beams in the roof are veiled by cobwebs. They are lovely, I think, gazing up at them with new eyes; they soften the hard lines of the rafters as grey hairs soften the lines on a middle-aged face. I no longer pull out grey hairs or sweep down cobwebs. As for the walls, it is true they looked forbidding at first. I felt cramped and enclosed by their blank faces. I wanted to knock holes in them, to give them another dimension with pictures or windows. So I dragged home from the beach grey arms of driftwood, worn satin-smooth by wind and sand. I gathered trailing green vines with floppy red-tipped leaves. I picked up the whitened skeletons of conch shells, their curious hollowed-out shapes faintly reminiscent of abstract sculpture. With these tacked to walls and propped up in corners, I am satisfied. I have a periscope out to the world. I have a window, a view, a point of flight from my sedentary base.

I am content. I sit down at my desk, a bare kitchen table with a blotter, a bottle of ink, a sand dollar to weight down one corner, a clam shell for a pen tray, the broken tip of a conch, pink-tinged, to finger, and a row of shells to set my thoughts spinning.

I love my sea-shell of a house. I wish I could live in it always. I wish I could transport it home. But I cannot. It will not hold a husband, five children and the necessities and trappings of daily life. I can only carry back my little channelled whelk. It will sit on my desk in Connecticut, to remind me of the ideal of a simplified life, to encourage me in the game I played on the beach. To ask how little, not how much, can I get along with. To say—is it necessary?—when I am tempted to add one more accumulation to my

Channelled Whelk

life, when I am pulled toward one more centrifugal activity.

Simplification of outward life is not enough. It is merely the outside. But I am starting with the outside. I am looking at the outside of a shell, the outside of my life—the shell. The complete answer is not to be found on the outside, in an outward mode of living. This is only a technique, a road to grace. The final answer, I know, is always inside. But the outside can give a clue, can help one to find the inside answer. One is free, like the hermit crab, to change one's shell.

Channelled whelk, I put you down again, but you have set my mind on a journey, up an inwardly winding spiral staircase of thought.

· 3 ·

MOON SHELL

This is a snail shell, round, full and glossy as a horse chestnut. Comfortable and compact, it sits curled up like a cat in the hollow of my hand. Milky and opaque, it has the pinkish bloom of the sky on a summer evening, ripening to rain. On its smooth symmetrical face is pencilled with precision a perfect spiral, winding inward to the pinpoint center of the shell, the tiny dark core of the apex, the pupil of the eye. It stares at me, this mysterious single eye—and I stare back.

Now it is the moon, solitary in the sky, full and round, replete with power. Now it is the eye of a cat that brushes noiselessly through long grass at night. Now it is an island, set in ever-widening circles of waves, alone, self-contained, serene.

How wonderful are islands! Islands in space, like this one I have come to, ringed about by miles of water, linked by no bridges, no cables, no telephones. An island from the world and the world's life. Islands in time, like this short vacation of mine. The past and the future are cut off; only the present remains. Existence in the present gives island living an extreme vividness and purity. One lives like a child or a saint in the immediacy of here and now. Every day, every act, is an island, washed by time and space, and has an island's completion. People too become like islands in such an atmosphere, self-contained, whole and serene; respecting other people's solitude, not intruding on their shores, standing back in reverence before the miracle of another individual. "No man is an island," said John Donne. I feel we are all islands—in a common sea.

We are all, in the last analysis, alone. And this basic state of solitude is not something we have any choice about. It is, as the poet Rilke says, "not something that one can take or leave. We *are* solitary. We may delude ourselves and act as though this were not so. That is all. But how much better it is to realize that we are so, yes, even to begin by assuming it. Naturally," he goes on to say, "we will turn giddy."

Naturally. How one hates to think of oneself as alone. How one avoids it. It seems to imply rejection or unpopularity. An early wallflower panic still clings to the word. One will be left, one fears, sitting in a straight-backed chair *alone,* while the popular girls are already chosen and spinning around the dance floor with their hot-palmed partners. We seem so frightened today of being alone that we never let it happen. Even if family, friends and movies should fail, there is still the radio or television to fill up the void. Women, who used to complain of loneliness, need never be alone any more. We can do our housework with soap-opera heroes at our side. Even day-dreaming was more creative than this; it demanded something of oneself and it fed the inner life. Now, instead of planting our solitude with our own dream blossoms, we choke the space with continuous music, chatter and companionship to which we do not even listen. It is simply there to fill the vacuum. When the noise stops there is no inner music to take its place. We must re-learn to be alone.

It is a difficult lesson to learn today—to leave one's friends and family and deliberately practice the art of solitude for an hour or a day or a week. For me, the break is the most difficult. Parting is inevitably painful, even for a short time. It is like an amputation, I feel. A limb is being torn off, without which I shall be unable to function. And yet, once it is done, I find there is a quality to being alone that is incredibly precious. Life rushes back into the void, richer, more vivid, fuller than before. It is as if in parting one did actually lose an arm. And then, like the star-fish, one grows it anew; one is whole again, complete and round—more whole, even, than before, when the other people had pieces of one.

Moon Shell

For a full day and two nights I have been alone. I lay on the beach under the stars at night alone. I made my breakfast alone. Alone I watched the gulls at the end of the pier, dip and wheel and dive for the scraps I threw them. A morning's work at my desk, and then, a late picnic lunch alone on the beach. And it seemed to me, separated from my own species, that I was nearer to others: the shy willet, nesting in the ragged tide-wash behind me; the sandpiper, running in little unfrightened steps down the shining beach rim ahead of me; the slowly flapping pelicans over my head, coasting down wind; the old gull, hunched up, grouchy, surveying the horizon. I felt a kind of impersonal kinship with them and a joy in that kinship. Beauty of earth and sea and air meant more to me. I was in harmony with it, melted into the universe, lost in it, as one is lost in a canticle of praise, swelling from an unknown crowd in a cathedral. "Praise ye the Lord, all ye fishes of the sea—all ye birds of the air—all ye children of men—Praise ye the Lord!"

Yes, I felt closer to my fellow men too, even in my solitude. For it is not physical solitude that actually separates one from other men, not physical isolation, but spiritual isolation. It is not the desert island nor the stony wilderness that cuts you from the people you love. It is the wilderness in the mind, the desert wastes in the heart through which one wanders lost and a stranger. When one is a stranger to oneself then one is estranged from others too. If one is out of touch with oneself, then one cannot touch others. How often in a large city, shaking hands with my friends, I have felt the wilderness stretching between us. Both of us were wandering in arid wastes, having lost the springs that nourished us—or having found them dry. Only when one is connected to one's own core is one connected to others, I am beginning to discover. And, for me, the core, the inner spring, can best be refound through solitude.

I walked far down the beach, soothed by the rhythm of the waves, the sun on my bare back and legs, the wind and mist from the spray on my hair. Into the waves and out like a sandpiper. And then home, drenched, drugged, reeling, full to the brim with my day alone; full like the moon before the night has taken a single nibble of it; full as a cup poured up to the lip. There is a quality to fullness that the Psalmist expressed: "My cup runneth over." Let no one come—I pray in sudden panic—I might spill myself away!

Is this then what happens to woman? She wants perpetually to spill herself away. All her instinct as a woman—the eternal nourisher of children, of men, of society—demands that she give. Her time, her energy, her creativeness drain out into these channels if there is any chance, any leak. Traditionally we are taught, and instinctively we long, to give where it is needed—and immediately. Eternally, woman spills herself away in driblets to the thirsty, seldom being allowed the time, the quiet, the peace, to let the pitcher fill up to the brim.

But why not, one may ask? What is wrong with woman's spilling herself away, since it is her function to give? Why am I, coming back from my perfect day at the beach, so afraid of losing my treasure? It is not just the artist in me. The artist, naturally, always resents giving himself in small drops. He must save up for the pitcher-full. No, it is also the woman in me who is so unexpectedly miserly.

Here is a strange paradox. Woman instinctively wants to give, yet resents giving herself in small pieces. Basically is this a conflict? Or is it an over-simplification of a many-stranded problem? I believe that what woman resents is not so much giving herself in pieces as giving herself purposelessly. What we fear is not so much that our energy may be leaking away through small outlets as that it may be going "down the drain." We do not see the results of our giving as concretely as man does in his work. In the job of home-keeping there is no raise from the boss, and sel-dom praise from others to show us we have hit the mark. Except for the child, woman's creation is so often invisible, especially today. We are working at an arrangement in form, of the myriad disparate details of housework, family routine and social life. It is a kind of intricate game of cat's-cradle we manipulate on our fingers, with invisible threads. How can one point to this constant tangle of household chores, errands and fragments of human relationships, as a creation? It is hard even to think of it as purposeful activity, so much of it is automatic. Woman herself begins to feel like a telephone exchange or a laundromat.

Purposeful giving is not as apt to deplete one's resources; it belongs to that natural order of giving that seems to renew itself even in the act of depletion. The more one gives, the more one has to give— like milk in the breast. In our early pioneer days and recently in war-time Europe, difficult as it was, woman's giving was purposeful, indispensable. Today, in our comparative comfort, many women hardly feel indispensable any more, either in the primitive struggle to survive or as the cultural font of the home. No longer fed by a feeling of indispensability or purposefulness, we are hungry, and not knowing what we are hungry for, we fill up the void with endless distractions, always at hand—unnecessary errands, compulsive duties, social niceties. And for the most part, to little purpose. Suddenly the spring is dry; the well is empty.

Hunger cannot, of course, be fed merely by a feeling of indispensability. Even purposeful giving must have some source that refills it. The milk in the breast must be replenished by food taken into the body. If it is woman's function to give, she must be replenished too. But how?

Solitude, says the moon shell. Every person, especially every woman, should be alone sometime during the year, some part of each week, and each day. How revolutionary that sounds and how impossible of attainment. To many women such a program seems quite out of reach. They have no extra income to spend on a vacation for themselves; no time left over from the weekly drudgery of housework for a day off; no energy after the daily cooking, cleaning and washing for even an hour of creative solitude.

Is this then only an economic problem? I do not think so. Every paid worker, no matter where in the economic scale, expects a day off a week and a vacation a year. By and large, mothers and housewives are the only workers who do not have regular time off. They are the great vacationless class. They rarely even complain of their lack, apparently not considering occasional time to themselves as a justifiable need.

Moon Shell

Herein lies one key to the problem. If women were convinced that a day off or an hour of solitude was a reasonable ambition, they would find a way of attaining it. As it is, they feel so unjustified in their demand that they rarely make the attempt. One has only to look at those women who actually have the economic means or the time and energy for solitude yet do not use it, to realize that the problem is not solely economic. It is more a question of inner convictions than of outer pressures, though, of course, the outer pressures are there and make it more difficult. As far as the search for solitude is concerned, we live in a negative atmosphere as invisible, as all-pervasive and as enervating as high humidity on an August afternoon. The world today does not understand, in either man or woman, the need to be alone.

How inexplicable it seems. Anything else will be accepted as a better excuse. If one sets aside time for a business appointment, a trip to the hairdresser, a social engagement or a shopping expedition, that time is accepted as inviolable. But if one says: I cannot come because that is my hour to be alone, one is considered rude, egotistical or strange. What a commentary on our civilization, when being alone is considered suspect; when one has to apologize for it, make excuses, hide the fact that one practices it—like a secret vice!

Actually these are among the most important times in one's life—when one is alone. Certain springs are tapped only when we are alone. The artist knows he must be alone to create; the writer, to work out his thoughts; the musician, to compose; the saint, to pray. But women need solitude in order to find again the true essence of themselves: that firm strand which will be the indispensable center of a whole web of human relationships. She must find that inner stillness which Charles Morgan describes as "the stilling of the soul within the activities of the mind and body so that it might be still as the axis of a revolving wheel is still."

This beautiful image is to my mind the one that women could hold before their eyes. This is an end toward which we could strive—to be the still axis within the revolving wheel of relationships, obligations and activities. Solitude alone is not the answer to this; it is only a step toward it, a mechanical aid, like the "room of one's own" demanded for women, before they could make their place in the world. The problem is not entirely in finding the room of one's own, the time alone, difficult and necessary as this is. The problem is more how to still the soul in the midst of its activities. In fact, the problem is how to feed the soul.

For it is the spirit of woman that is going dry, not the mechanics that are wanting. Mechanically, woman has gained in the past generation. Certainly in America, our lives are easier, freer, more open to opportunities, thanks—among other things—to the Feminist battles. The room of one's own, the hour alone are now more possible in a wider economic class than ever before. But these hard-won prizes are insufficient because we have not yet learned how to use them. The Feminists did not look that far ahead; they laid down no rules of conduct. For them it was enough to demand the privileges. The exploration of their use, as in all pioneer movements, was left open to the women who would follow. And woman today is still searching. We are aware of our hunger and needs, but still ignorant of what will satisfy them. With our garnered free time, we are more apt to drain our creative springs than to refill them. With our pitchers, we attempt sometimes to water a field, not a garden. We throw ourselves indiscriminately into committees and causes. Not knowing how to feed the spirit, we try to muffle its demands in distractions. Instead of stilling the center, the axis of the wheel, we add more centrifugal activities to our lives—which tend to throw us off balance.

Mechanically we have gained, in the last generation, but spiritually we have, I think, unwittingly lost. In other times, women had in their lives more forces which centered them whether or not they realized it; sources which nourished them whether or not they consciously went to these springs. Their very seclusion in the home gave them time alone. Many of their duties were conducive to a quiet contemplative drawing together of the self. They had more creative tasks to perform. Nothing feeds the center so much as creative work, even humble kinds like cooking and sewing. Baking bread, weaving

Moon Shell

cloth, putting up preserves, teaching and singing to children, must have been far more nourishing than being the family chauffeur or shopping at supermarkets, or doing housework with mechanical aids. The art and craft of housework has diminished; much of the time-consuming drudgery—despite modern advertising to the contrary—remains. In housework, as in the rest of life, the curtain of mechanization has come down between the mind and the hand.

The church, too, has always been a great centering force for women. Through what ages women have had that quiet hour, free of interruption, to draw themselves together. No wonder woman has been the mainstay of the church. Here were the advantages of the room of her own, the time alone, the quiet, the peace, all rolled into one and sanctioned by the approval of both family and community. Here no one could intrude with a careless call, "Mother," "Wife," "Mistress." Here, finally and more deeply, woman was whole, not split into a thousand functions. She was able to give herself completely in that hour in worship, in prayer, in communion, and be completely accepted. And in that giving and acceptance she was renewed; the springs were refilled.

The church is still a great centering force for men and women, more needed than ever before—as its increasing membership shows. But are those who attend as ready to give themselves or to receive its message as they used to be? Our daily life does not prepare us for contemplation. How can a single weekly hour of church, helpful as it may be, counteract the many daily hours of distraction that surround it? If we had our contemplative hour at home we might be readier to give ourselves at church and find ourselves more completely renewed. For the need for renewal is still there. The desire to be accepted whole, the desire to be seen as an individual, not as a collection of functions, the desire to give oneself completely and purposefully pursues us always, and has its part in pushing us into more and more distractions, illusory love affairs or the haven of hospitals and doctors' offices.

The answer is not in going back, in putting woman in the home and giving her the broom and the needle again. A number of mechanical aids save us time and energy. But neither is the answer in dissipating our time and energy in more purposeless occupations, more accumulations which supposedly simplify life but actually burden it, more possessions which we have not time to use or appreciate, more diversions to fill up the void.

In other words, the answer is not in the feverish pursuit of centrifugal activities which only lead in the end to fragmentation. Woman's life today is tending more and more toward the state William James describes so well in the German word, "Zerrissenheit—torn-to-pieces-hood." She cannot live perpetually in "Zerrissenheit." She will be shattered into a thousand pieces. On the contrary, she must consciously encourage those pursuits which oppose the centrifugal forces of today. Quiet time alone, contemplation, prayer, music, a centering line of thought or reading, of study or work. It can be physical or intellectual or artistic, any creative life proceeding from oneself. It need not be an enormous project or a great work. But it should be something of one's own. Arranging a bowl of flowers in the morning can give a sense of quiet in a crowded day—like writing a poem, or saying a prayer. What matters is that one be for a time inwardly attentive.

Solitude, says the moon shell. Center-down, say the Quaker saints. To the possession of the self the way is inward, says Plotinus. The cell of self-knowledge is the stall in which the pilgrim must be reborn, says St. Catherine of Siena. Voices from the past. In fact, these are pursuits and virtues of the past. But done in another way today because done consciously, aware, with eyes open. Not done as before, as part of the pattern of the time. Not done because everyone else is doing them; almost no one is doing them. Revolutionary, in fact, because almost every trend and pressure, every voice from the outside is against this new way of inward living.

Woman must be the pioneer in this turning inward for strength. In a sense she has always been the pioneer. Less able, until the last generation, to escape into outward activities, the very limitations of her life forced her to look inward. And from looking inward she gained an inner strength which man in his out-

Moon Shell

ward active life did not as often find. But in our recent efforts to emancipate ourselves, to prove ourselves the equal of man, we have, naturally enough perhaps, been drawn into competing with him in his outward activities, to the neglect of our own inner springs. Why have we been seduced into abandoning this timeless inner strength of woman for the temporal outer strength of man? This outer strength of man is essential to the pattern, but even here the reign of purely outer strength and purely outward solutions seems to be waning today. Men too are being forced to look inward—to find inner solutions as well as outer ones. Perhaps this change marks a new stage of maturity for modern extrovert, activist, materialistic Western man. Can it be that he is beginning to realize that the kingdom of heaven is within?

. . .

Moon shell, who named you? Some intuitive woman I like to think. I shall give you another name—Island shell. I cannot live forever on my island. But I can take you back to my desk in Connecticut. You will sit there and fasten your single eye upon me. You will make me think, with your smooth circles winding inward to the tiny core, of the island I lived on for a few weeks. You will say to me "solitude." You will remind me that I must try to be alone for part of each year, even a week or a few days; and for part of each day, even for an hour or a few minutes in order to keep my core, my center, my island-quality. You will remind me that unless I keep the island-quality intact somewhere within me, I will have little to give my husband, my children, my friends or the world at large. You will remind me that woman must be still as the axis of a wheel in the midst of her activities; that she must be the pioneer in achieving this stillness, not only for her own salvation, but for the salvation of family life, of society, perhaps even of our civilization.

· 4 ·

DOUBLE-SUNRISE

This shell was a gift; I did not find it. It was handed to me by a friend. It is unusual on the island. One does not often come across such a perfect double-sunrise shell. Both halves of this delicate bivalve are exactly matched. Each side, like the wing of a butterfly, is marked with the same pattern; translucent white, except for three rosy rays that fan out from the golden hinge binding the two together. I hold two sunrises between my thumb and finger. Smooth, whole, unblemished shell, I wonder how its fragile perfection survived the breakers on the beach.

It is unusual; yet it was given to me freely. People are like that here. Strangers smile at you on the beach, come up and offer you a shell, for no reason, lightly, and then go by and leave you alone again. Nothing is demanded of you in payment, no social rite expected, no tie established. It was a gift, freely offered, freely taken, in mutual trust. People smile at you here, like children, sure that you will not rebuff them, that you will smile back. And you do, because you know it will involve nothing. The smile, the act, the relationship is hung in space, in the immediacy and purity of the present; suspended on the still point of here and now; balanced there, on a shaft of air, like a seagull.

The pure relationship, how beautiful it is! How easily it is damaged, or weighed down with irrelevancies—not even irrelevancies, just life itself, the accumulations of life and of time. For the first part of every relationship is pure, whether it be with friend or lover, husband or child. It is pure, simple and unencumbered. It is like the artist's vision before he has to discipline it into form, or like the flower of love before it has ripened to the firm but heavy fruit of responsibility. Every relationship seems simple at its start. The simplicity of first love, or friendliness, the mutuality of first sympathy seems, at its initial appearance—even if merely in exciting conversation across a dinner table—to be a self-enclosed world. Two people listening to each other, two shells meeting each other, making one world between them. There are no others in the perfect unity of that instant, no other people or things or interests. It is free of ties or claims, unburdened by responsibilities, by worry about the future or debts to the past.

And then how swiftly, how inevitably the perfect unity is invaded; the relationship changes; it becomes complicated, encumbered by its contact with the world. I believe this is true in most relationships, with friends, with husband or wife, and with one's children. But it is the marriage relationship in which the changing pattern is shown up most clearly because it is the deepest one and the most arduous to maintain; and because, somehow, we mistakenly feel that failure to maintain its exact original pattern is tragedy.

It is true, of course, the original relationship is very beautiful. Its self-enclosed perfection wears the freshness of a spring morning. Forgetting about the summer to come, one often feels one would like to prolong the spring of early love, when two people stand as individuals, without past or future, facing each other. One resents any change, even though one knows that transformation is natural and part of the process of life and its evolution. Like its parallel in physical passion, the early ecstatic stage of a relationship cannot continue always at the same pitch of intensity. It moves to another phase of growth which one should not dread, but welcome as one welcomes summer after spring. But there is also a dead weight accumulation, a coating of false values, habits and burdens which blights life. It is this smothering coat that needs constantly to be stripped off, in life as well as in relationships.

Both men and women feel the change in the early relationship and hunger nostalgically for its original

pattern as life goes on and becomes more complicated. For inevitably, as the relationship grows, both
men and women, at least to some degree, are drawn
into their more specialized and functional roles: man,
into his less personal work in the world; woman, into
her traditional obligations with family and household. In both fields, functional relationships tend to
take the place of the early all-absorbing personal one.
But woman refinds in a limited form with each new
child, something resembling, at least in its absorption,
the early pure relationship. In the sheltered simplicity
of the first days after a baby is born, one sees again the
magical closed circle, the miraculous sense of two
people existing only for each other, the tranquil sky
reflected on the face of the mother nursing her child.
It is, however, only a brief interlude and not a substitute for the original more complete relationship.

But though both men and women are absorbed in
their specialized roles and each misses something of
the early relationship, there are great differences in
their needs. While man, in his realm, has less chance
for personal relations than woman, he may have more

opportunity for giving himself creatively in work. Woman, on the other hand, has more chance for personal relations, but these do not give her a sense of her creative identity, the individual who has something of her own to say or to give. With each partner hungry for different reasons and each misunderstanding the other's needs, it is easy to fall apart or into late love affairs. The temptation is to blame the situation on the other person and to accept the easy solution that a new and more understanding partner will solve everything.

But neither woman nor man are likely to be fed by another relationship which seems easier because it is in an earlier stage. Such a love affair cannot really bring back a sense of identity. Certainly, one has the illusion that one will find oneself in being loved for what one really is, not for a collection of functions. But can one actually find oneself in someone else? In someone else's love? Or even in the mirror someone else holds up for one? I believe that true identity is found, as Eckhart once said, by "going into one's own ground and knowing oneself." It is found in creative activity springing from within. It is found, paradoxically, when one loses oneself. One must lose one's life to find it. Woman can best refind herself by losing herself in some kind of creative activity of her own. Here she will be able to refind her strength, the strength she needs to look and work at the second half of the problem—the neglected pure relationship. Only a refound person can refind a personal relationship.

But can the pure relationship of the sunrise shell be refound once it has become obscured? Obviously some relationships can never be recovered. It is not just a question of different needs to be understood and filled. In their changing roles the two partners may have grown in different directions or at different rates of speed. A brief double-sunrise episode may have been all they could achieve. It was an end in itself and not a foundation for a deeper relation. In a growing relationship, however, the original essence is not lost but merely buried under the impedimenta of life. The core of reality is still there and needs only to be uncovered and reaffirmed.

Gift from the Sea

One way of rediscovering the double-sunrise is to duplicate some of its circumstances. Husband and wife can and should go off on vacations alone and also on vacations alone *together*. For if it is possible that woman can find herself by having a vacation alone, it is equally possible that the original relationship can sometimes be refound by having a vacation alone *together*. Most married couples have felt the unexpected joy of one of these vacations. How wonderful it was to leave the children, the house, the job and all the obligations of daily life; to go out together, whether for a month or a weekend or even just a night in an inn by themselves. How surprising it was to find the miracle of the sunrise repeated. There was the sudden pleasure of having breakfast alone with the man one fell in love with. Here at the small table, are only two people facing each other. How the table at home has grown! And how distracting it is, with four or five children, a telephone ringing in the hall, two or three school buses to catch, not to speak of the commuter's train. How all this separates one from one's husband and clogs up the pure relationship. But sitting at a table alone opposite each other, what is there to separate one? Nothing but a coffee pot, corn muffins and marmalade. A simple enough pleasure, surely, to have breakfast alone with one's husband, but how seldom married people in the midst of life achieve it.

Actually, I believe this temporary return to the pure relationship holds good for one's children too. If only, I think, playing with my sunrise shell—if only we could have each of our children alone, not just for part of each day, but for part of each month, each year. Would they not be happier, stronger and, in the end, more independent because more secure? Does each child not secretly long for the pure relationship he once had with the mother, when he was "The Baby," when the nursery doors were shut and she was feeding him at her breast—*alone*? And if we were able to put into practice this belief and spend more time with each child alone—would he not only gain in security and strength, but also learn an important first lesson in his adult relationship?

We all wish to be loved alone. "Don't sit under the

apple tree with anyone else but me," runs the old popular song. Perhaps, as Auden says in his poem, this is a fundamental error in mankind.

> For the error bred in the bone
> Of each woman and each man
> Craves what it cannot have,
> Not universal love
> But to be loved alone.

Is it such a sin? In discussing this verse with an Indian philosopher, I had an illuminating answer. "It is all right to wish to be loved alone," he said, "mutuality is the essence of love. There cannot be others in mutuality. It is only in the time-sense that it is wrong. It is when we desire *continuity* of being loved alone that we go wrong." For not only do we insist on believing romantically in the "one-and-only"—the one-and-only love, the one-and-only mate, the one-and-only mother, the one-and-only security—we wish the "one-and-only" to be permanent, ever-present and continuous. The desire for continuity of being-loved-alone seems to me "the error bred in the bone" of man.

Double-Sunrise

For "there is no one-and-only," as a friend of mine once said in a similar discussion, "there are just one-and-only moments."

The one-and-only moments are justified. The return to them, even if temporarily, is valid. The moment over the marmalade and muffins is valid; the moment feeding the child at the breast is valid; the moment racing with him later on the beach is valid. Finding shells together, polishing chestnuts, sharing one's treasures:—all these moments of together-aloneness are valid, but not permanent.

One comes in the end to realize that there is no permanent pure-relationship and there should not be. It is not even something to be desired. The pure relationship is limited, in space and in time. In its essence it implies exclusion. It excludes the rest of life, other relationships, other sides of personality, other responsibilities, other possibilities in the future. It excludes growth. The other children are there clamoring outside the closed nursery door. One loves them too. The telephone rings in the next room. One also wants to talk to friends. When the muffins are cleared away, one must think of the next meal or the next day. These are realities too, not to be excluded. Life must go on. That does not mean it is a waste of time to recreate for brief holiday periods together-alone experiences. On the contrary, these one-and-only moments are both refreshing and rewarding. The light shed over the small breakfast table illumines the day, many days. The race on the beach together renews one's youth like a dip in the sea. But we are no longer children; life is not a beach. There is no pattern here for permanent return, only for refreshment.

One learns to accept the fact that no permanent return is possible to an old form of relationship; and, more deeply still, that there is no holding of a relationship to a single form. This is not tragedy but part of the ever-recurrent miracle of life and growth. All living relationships are in process of change, of expansion, and must perpetually be building themselves new forms. But there is no single fixed form to express such a changing relationship. There are perhaps different forms for each successive stage; different shells I might put in a row on my desk to suggest the different stages of marriage—or indeed of any relationship.

Double-Sunrise

My double-sunrise shell comes first. It is a valid image, I think, for the first stage: two flawless halves bound together with a single hinge, meeting each other at every point, the dawn of a new day spreading on each face. It is a world to itself. Is this not what the poets have always been attempting to describe?

> And now good-morrow to our waking souls
> Which watch not one another out of fear;
> For love all love of other sights controls,
> And makes one little room an everywhere.
> Let sea-discoverers to new worlds have gone,
> Let maps to other, worlds on worlds have shown,
> Let us possess one world, each hath one, and is one.

It is, however, a "little room," that Donne describes, a small world, that must be inevitably and happily outgrown. Beautiful, fragile, fleeting, the sunrise shell; but not, for all that, illusory. Because it is not lasting, let us not fall into the cynic's trap and call it an illusion. Duration is not a test of true or false. The day of the dragon-fly or the night of the Saturnid moth is not invalid simply because that phase in its life cycle is brief. Validity need have no relation to time, to duration, to continuity. It is on another plane, judged by other standards. It relates to the actual moment in time and place. "And what is actual is actual only for one time and only for one place." The sunrise shell has the eternal validity of all beautiful and fleeting things.

· 5 ·

OYSTER BED

B ut surely we *do* demand duration and continuity of relationships, at least of marriage. That is what marriage is, isn't it—continuity of a relationship? Of course, but not necessarily continuity in one single form or stage; not necessarily continuity in the double-sunrise stage. There are other shells to help me, to put in the row on my desk. Here is one I picked up yesterday. Not rare; there are many of them on the beach and yet each one is individual. You never find two alike. Each is fitted and formed by its own life and struggle to survive. It is an oyster, with small shells clinging to its humped back. Sprawling and uneven, it has the irregularity of something growing. It looks rather like the house of a big family, pushing out one addition after another to hold its teeming life—here a sleeping porch for the children, and there a veranda for the play-pen; here a garage for the extra car and there a shed for the bicycles. It amuses me because it seems so much like my life at the moment, like most women's lives in the middle years of marriage. It is untidy, spread out in all directions, heavily encrusted with accumulations and, in its living state—this one is empty and cast up by the sea—firmly imbedded on its rock.

Yes, I believe the oyster shell is a good one to express the middle years of marriage. It suggests the struggle of life itself. The oyster has fought to have that place on the rock to which it has fitted itself perfectly and to which it clings tenaciously. So most couples in the growing years of marriage struggle to achieve a place in the world. It is a physical and material battle first of all, for a home, for children, for a place in their particular society. In the midst of such a life there is not much time to sit facing one another over a breakfast table. In these years one recognizes the truth of Saint-Exupéry's line: "Love does not consist in gazing at each other (one perfect sunrise gazing at another!) but in looking outward together in the same direction." For, in fact, man and woman are not only *looking* outward in the same direction; they are *working* outward. (Observe the steady encroachment of the oyster bed over the rock.) Here one forms ties, roots, a firm base. (Try and pry an oyster from its ledge!) Here one makes oneself part of the community of men, of human society.

Here the bonds of marriage are formed. For marriage, which is always spoken of as a bond, becomes actually, in this stage, many bonds, many strands, of different texture and strength, making up a web that is taut and firm. The web is fashioned of love. Yes, but many kinds of love: romantic love first, then a slow-growing devotion and, playing through these, a

constantly rippling companionship. It is made of loy-
alties, and interdependencies, and shared experiences.
It is woven of memories of meetings and conflicts; of
triumphs and disappointments. It is a web of communication, a common language, and the acceptance of
lack of language too; a knowledge of likes and dislikes,
of habits and reactions, both physical and mental. It is
a web of instincts and intuitions, and known and
unknown exchanges. The web of marriage is made by
propinquity, in the day-to-day living side by side,
looking outward and working outward in the same
direction. It is woven in space and in time of the substance of life itself.

But the bond—the bond of romantic love is something else. It has so little to do with propinquity or
habit or space or time or life itself. It leaps across all
of them, like a rainbow—or a glance. It is the bond of
romantic love which fastens the double-sunrise shell,
only one bond, one hinge. And if that fragile link is
snapped in the storm, what will hold the halves to
each other? In the oyster stage of marriage, romantic
love is only one of the many bonds that make up the

intricate and enduring web that two people have built together.

I am very fond of the oyster shell. It is humble and awkward and ugly. It is slate-colored and unsymmetrical. Its form is not primarily beautiful but functional. I make fun of its knobbiness. Sometimes I resent its burdens and excrescences. But its tireless adaptability and tenacity draw my astonished admiration and sometimes even my tears. And it is comfortable in its familiarity, its homeliness, like old garden gloves which have moulded themselves perfectly to the shape of the hand. I do not like to put it down. I will not want to leave it.

But is it the permanent symbol of marriage? Should it—any more than the double-sunrise shell—last forever? The tide of life recedes. The house, with its bulging sleeping porches and sheds, begins little by little to empty. The children go away to school and then to marriage and lives of their own. Most people by middle age have attained, or ceased to struggle to attain, their place in the world. That terrific tenacity to life, to place, to people, to material surroundings and accumulations—is it as necessary as it was when one was struggling for one's security or the security of one's children? Many of the physical struggles have ceased, due either to success or to failure. Does the shell need to be so welded to its rock? Married couples are apt to find themselves in middle age, high and dry in an outmoded shell, in a fortress which has outlived its function. What is one to do—die of atrophy in an outstripped form? Or move on to another form, other experiences?

Perhaps, someone will suggest, this is the moment to go back to the simple self-enclosed world of the sunrise shell? Alone at last again over the muffins and the marmalade! No, one cannot go back to that tightly closed world. One has grown too big, too many-sided, for that rigidly symmetrical shell. I am not sure that one has not grown too big for any shell at all.

Perhaps middle age is, or should be, a period of shedding shells; the shell of ambition, the shell of material accumulations and possessions, the shell of the ego. Perhaps one can shed at this stage in life as one sheds in beach-living; one's pride, one's false ambitions, one's mask, one's armor. Was that armor not put on to protect one from the competitive world? If one ceases to compete, does one need it? Perhaps one can at last in middle age, if not earlier, be completely oneself. And what a liberation that would be!

It is true that the adventures of youth are less open to us. Most of us cannot, at this point, start a new career or raise a new family. Many of the physical, material and worldly ambitions are less attainable than they were twenty years ago. But is this not often a relief? "I no longer worry about being the belle of Newport," a beautiful woman, who had become a talented artist, once said to me. And I always liked that Virginia Woolf hero who meets middle age admitting: "Things have dropped from me. I have outlived certain desires . . . I am not so gifted as at one time seemed likely. Certain things lie beyond my scope. I shall never understand the harder problems of philosophy. Rome is the limit of my travelling . . . I shall never see savages in Tahiti spearing fish by the light of a blazing cresset, or a lion spring in the jungle, or a naked man eating raw flesh . . ." (Thank God! you can hear him adding under his breath.)

The primitive, physical, functional pattern of the

morning of life, the active years before forty or fifty, is outlived: But there is still the afternoon opening up, which one can spend not in the feverish pace of the morning but in having time at last for those intellectual, cultural and spiritual activities that were pushed aside in the heat of the race. We Americans, with our terrific emphasis on youth, action and material success, certainly tend to belittle the afternoon of life and even to pretend it never comes. We push the clock back and try to prolong the morning, overreaching and overstraining ourselves in the unnatural effort. We do not succeed, of course. We cannot compete with our sons and daughters. And what a struggle it is to race with these overactive and under-wise adults! In our breathless attempts we often miss the flowering that waits for afternoon.

For is it not possible that middle age can be looked upon as a period of second flowering, second growth, even a kind of second adolescence? It is true that society in general does not help one accept this interpretation of the second half of life. And therefore this period of expanding is often tragically misunderstood.

Oyster Bed

Many people never climb above the plateau of forty-to-fifty. The signs that presage growth, so similar, it seems to me, to those in early adolescence: discontent, restlessness, doubt, despair, longing, are interpreted falsely as signs of decay. In youth one does not as often misinterpret the signs; one accepts them, quite rightly, as growing pains. One takes them seriously, listens to them, follows where they lead. One is afraid. Naturally. Who is not afraid of pure space—that breathtaking empty space of an open door? But despite fear, one goes through to the room beyond.

But in middle age, because of the false assumption that it is a period of decline, one interprets these life-signs, paradoxically, as signs of approaching death. Instead of facing them, one runs away; one escapes—into depressions, nervous breakdowns, drink, love affairs or frantic, thoughtless, fruitless overwork. Anything, rather than face them. Anything, rather than stand still and learn from them. One tries to cure the signs of growth, to exorcise them, as if they were devils, when really they might be angels of annunciation.

Angels of annunciation of what? Of a new stage in

living when, having shed many of the physical struggles, the worldly ambitions, the material encumbrances of active life, one might be free to fulfill the neglected side of one's self. One might be free for growth of mind, heart and talent; free at last for spiritual growth; free of the clamping sunrise shell. Beautiful as it was, it was still a closed world one had to outgrow. And the time may come when—comfortable and adaptable as it is— one may outgrow even the oyster shell.

· 6 ·

ARGONAUTA

There are in the beach-world certain rare creatures, the "Argonauta" (Paper Nautilus), who are not fastened to their shell at all. It is actually a cradle for the young, held in the arms of the mother argonaut who floats with it to the surface, where the eggs hatch and the young swim away. Then the mother argonaut leaves her shell and starts another life. I am fascinated by this image of the argonaut, whose temporary dwelling I have seen only as the treasure of a specialist's collection. Almost transparent, delicately fluted like a Greek column, this narcissus-white snail shell is feather light as some coracle of ancient times, ready to set sail across unknown seas. It was named, the book tells me, for the fabled ships of Jason that went in search of the Golden Fleece. Sailors consider these shells a sign of fair weather and favorable winds.

Lovely shell, lovely image—I am tempted to play with it in my mind. Is this the symbol for another stage in relationships? Can we middle-aged argonauts when we outgrow the oyster bed, look forward to the freedom of the nautilus who has left its shell for the open seas? But what does the open sea hold for us? We cannot believe that the second half of life promises "fair weather and favorable winds." What golden fleece is there for the middle-aged?

In speaking of the argonauta one might as well admit one has left the usual shell collections. A double-sunrise shell, an oyster bed—these are common knowledge to most of us. We recognize them; we know about them; they are part of our daily life and the lives of others around us. But with this rare and delicate vessel, we have left the well-tracked beaches of proven facts and experiences. We are adventuring in the chartless seas of imagination.

Is the golden fleece that awaits us some kind of new freedom for growth? And in this new freedom, is there any place for a relationship? I believe there is, after the oyster bed, an opportunity for the best relationship of all: not a limited, mutually exclusive one, like the sunrise shell; and not a functional, dependent one, as in the oyster bed; but the meeting of two whole fully developed people as persons. It would be, to borrow a definition of the Scottish philosopher, MacMurray, a fully personal relationship, that is, "a type of relationship into which people enter as persons with the whole of themselves." "Personal relationships," he goes on to explain, ". . . have no ulterior motive. They are not based on particular interests. They do not serve partial and limited ends. Their value lies entirely in themselves and for the same reason transcends all other values. And that is because they are relations of persons as persons."

This relationship of "persons as persons" was prophetically hinted at by the German poet, Rilke, almost fifty years ago. He foresaw a great change in the relationships between men and women, which he hoped in the future would no longer follow the traditional patterns of submission and domination or of possession and competition. He described a state in which there would be space and freedom for growth, and in which each partner would be the means of releasing the other. "A relation," he concludes, "that is meant to be of one human being to another, . . . And this more human love (that will fulfill itself, infinitely considerate and gentle, and good and clear in binding and releasing) will resemble that which we are with struggle and endeavor preparing, the love that consists in this, that two solitudes protect and touch and greet each other."

But this new relationship of persons as persons, this more human love, this two solitudes conception is not something that comes easily. It must have grown, like all firm-rooted growth, slowly. It perhaps can only follow a long development in the history of human civilization and individually in each human being's life. Such a stage in life, it would seem to me, must come not as a gift or a lucky accident, but as part of an evolutionary process, an achievement which could only follow certain important developments in each partner.

It cannot be reached until woman—individually and as a sex—has herself come of age, a maturing process we are witnessing today. In this undertaking she must work alone and cannot count on much help from the outsider, eager as he may be in pointing out the way. There are many signs of interest in the new woman today, chiefly in the form of mechanistic studies of her as a female animal. Of course it is necessary and helpful for woman to understand and accept her sexual needs and habits but it is only one side of a very complex problem. One cannot expect statistics on her physical reactions to add much knowledge or nourishment to her inner life, to her basic relation to herself or to her long postponed hope and right, as a human being, to be creative in other ways besides the purely physical one.

Gift from the Sea

Woman must come of age by herself. This is the essence of "coming of age"—to learn how to stand alone. She must learn not to depend on another, nor to feel she must prove her strength by competing with another. In the past, she has swung between these two opposite poles of dependence and competition, of Victorianism and Feminism. Both extremes throw her off balance; neither is the center, the true center of being a whole woman. She must find her true center alone. She must become whole. She must, it seems to me, as a prelude to any "two solitudes" relationship, follow the advice of the poet to become "world to oneself for another's sake."

In fact, I wonder if both man and woman must not accomplish this heroic feat. Must not man also become world to himself? Must he not also expand the neglected sides of his personality; the art of inward looking that he has seldom had time for in his active outward-going life; the personal relationships which he has not had as much chance to enjoy; the so-called feminine qualities, aesthetic, emotional, cultural and spiritual, which he has been too rushed to fully develop. Perhaps both men and women in America may hunger, in our material, outward, active, masculine culture, for the supposedly feminine qualities of heart, mind and spirit— qualities which are actually neither masculine nor feminine, but simply human qualities that have been neglected. It is growth along these lines that will make us whole, and will enable the individual to become world to himself.

And this greater wholeness in each person, this being "world to oneself," does this not mean greater self-sufficiency and therefore, inevitably, greater separation between man and woman? With growth, it is true, comes differentiation and separation, in the sense that the unity of the tree-trunk differentiates as it grows and spreads into limbs, branches and leaves. But the tree is still one, and its different and separate parts contribute to one another. The two separate worlds or the two solitudes will surely have more to give each other than when each was a meager half. "A complete sharing between two people is an impossibility," writes Rilke, "and whenever it seems, nevertheless, to exist, it is a narrowing, a mutual agreement which robs either one member or both of his fullest freedom and development. But, once the realization is accepted that, even between the closest human beings, infinite distances continue to exist, a wonderful living side by side can grow up, if they succeed in loving the distance between them which makes it possible for each to see the other whole and against a wide sky!"

This is a beautiful image, but who can achieve it in actual life? Where has one seen such a marriage except in a poet's correspondence? It is true that Rilke's two solitudes or MacMurray's fully personal relationship are as yet somewhat theoretical concepts. But theory precedes exploration; we must use any signposts that exist to help us through the wilderness. For we are, actually, pioneers trying to find a new path through the maze of tradition, convention and dogma. Our efforts are part of the struggle to mature the conception of relationships between men and women—in fact all relationships. In such a light, every advance in understanding has value. Every step, even a tentative one, counts. And though we may seldom come upon a perfect argonauta life cycle, we have all had glimpses of them, even in our own lives for brief periods. And these brief experiences give us insight into what the new relation might be.

On this island I have had such a glimpse into the life of the argonauta. After my week alone I have had a week of living with my sister. I will take from it one day. I shall examine it, set it before me as I have set the shells on my desk. I shall turn it around like a shell, testing and analyzing its good points. Not that my life will ever become like this day—a perfect one plucked out of a holiday week; there are no perfect lives. The relation of two sisters is not that of a man and a woman. But it can illustrate the essence of relationships. The light shed by any good relationship illuminates all relationships. And one perfect day can give clues for a more perfect life—the mythical life, maybe, of the argonauta.

· · ·

We wake in the same small room from the deep sleep of good children, to the soft sound of wind through the casuarina trees and the gentle sleep-breathing rhythm of waves on the shore. We run bare-legged to the beach, which lies smooth, flat and glistening with fresh wet shells after the night's tides. The morning swim has the nature of a blessing to me, a baptism, a rebirth to the beauty and wonder of the world. We run back tingling to hot coffee on our small back porch. Two kitchen chairs and a child's table between us fill the stoop on which we sit. With legs in the sun we laugh and plan our day.

We wash the dishes lightly to no system, for there are not enough to matter. We work easily and instinctively together, not bumping into each other as we go back and forth about our tasks. We talk as we sweep, as we dry, as we put away, discussing a person or a poem or a memory. And since our communication seems more important to us than our chores, the chores are done without thinking.

And then to work, behind closed doors neither of us would want to invade. What release to write so that one forgets oneself, forgets one's companion, forgets where one is or what one is going to do next—to be drenched in work as one is drenched in sleep or in the sea. Pencils and pads and curling blue sheets alive with letters heap up on the desk. And then, pricked by hunger, we rise at last in a daze, for a late lunch. Reeling a little from our intense absorption, we come back with relief to the small chores of getting lunch, as if they were lifelines to reality—as if we had indeed almost drowned in the sea of intellectual work and welcomed the firm ground of physical action under our feet.

After an hour or so of practical jobs and errands we are ready to leave them again. Out onto the beach for the afternoon where we are swept clean of duties, of the particular, of the practical. We walk up the beach in silence, but in harmony, as the sandpipers ahead of us move like a corps of ballet dancers keeping time to some interior rhythm inaudible to us. Intimacy is blown away. Emotions are carried out to sea. We are even free of thoughts, at least of their articulation; clean and bare as whitened driftwood; empty as shells, ready to be filled up again with the impersonal sea and sky and wind. A long afternoon soaking up the outer world.

Gift from the Sea

And when we are heavy and relaxed as the seaweed under our feet, we return at dusk to the warmth and intimacy of our cottage. We sip sherry at leisure in front of a fire. We start supper and we talk. Evening is the time for conversation. Morning is for mental work, I feel, the habit of school-days persisting in me. Afternoon is for physical tasks, the out-of-door jobs. But evening is for sharing, for communication. Is it the uninterrupted dark expanse of the night after the bright segmented day, that frees us to each other? Or does the infinite space and infinite darkness dwarf and chill us, turning us to seek small human sparks?

Communication—but not for too long. Because good communication is stimulating as black coffee, and just as hard to sleep after. Before we sleep we go out again into the night. We walk up the beach under the stars. And when we are tired of walking, we lie flat on the sand under a bowl of stars. We feel stretched, expanded to take in their compass. They pour into us until we are filled with stars, up to the brim.

This is what one thirsts for, I realize, after the smallness of the day, of work, of details, of intimacy—

even of communication, one thirsts for the magnitude and universality of a night full of stars, pouring into one like a fresh tide.

And then at last, from the immensity of interstellar space, we swing down to a particular beach. We walk back to the lights of the cottage glowing from the dark mist of trees. Small, safe, warm and welcoming, we recognize our pinpoint human matchlight against the mammoth chaos of the dark. Back again to our good child's sleep.

. . .

What a wonderful day, I think, turning it around in my hand to its starting point again. What has made it so perfect? Is there not some clue here in the pattern of this day? To begin with, it is a pattern of freedom. Its setting has not been cramped in space or time. An island, curiously enough, gives a limitless feeling of both. Nor has the day been limited in kinds of activity. It has a natural balance of physical, intellectual and social life. It has an easy unforced rhythm. Work is not deformed by pressure. Relationship is not strangled by claims. Intimacy is tempered by lightness of touch. We have moved through our day like dancers, not needing to touch more than lightly because we were instinctively moving to the same rhythm.

A good relationship has a pattern like a dance and is built on some of the same rules. The partners do not need to hold on tightly, because they move confidently in the same pattern, intricate but gay and swift and free, like a country dance of Mozart's. To touch heavily would be to arrest the pattern and freeze the movement, to check the endlessly changing beauty of its unfolding. There is no place here for the possessive clutch, the clinging arm, the heavy hand; only the barest touch in passing. Now arm in arm, now face to face, now back to back—it does not matter which. Because they know they are partners moving to the same rhythm, creating a pattern together, and being invisibly nourished by it.

The joy of such a pattern is not only the joy of creation or the joy of participation, it is also the joy of living in the moment. Lightness of touch and living in the moment are intertwined. One cannot dance well unless one is completely in time with the music, not leaning back to the last step or pressing forward to the next one, but poised directly on the present step as it comes. Perfect poise on the beat is what gives good dancing its sense of ease, of timelessness, of the eternal. It is what Blake was speaking of when he wrote:

> *He who bends to himself a joy*
> *Doth the wingèd life destroy,*
> *But he who kisses the joy as it flies*
> *Lives in Eternity's sunrise.*

The dancers who are perfectly in time never destroy "the wingèd life" in each other or in themselves.

But how does one learn this technique of the dance? Why is it so difficult? What makes us hesitate and stumble? It is fear, I think, that makes one cling nostalgically to the last moment or clutch greedily toward the next. Fear destroys "the wingèd life." But how to exorcise it? It can only be exorcised by its opposite, love. When the heart is flooded with love there is no room in it for fear, for doubt, for hesitation. And it is this lack of fear that makes for the dance. When each partner loves so completely that he has forgotten to ask himself whether or not he is loved in return; when he only knows that he loves and is moving to its music—then, and then only, are two people able to dance perfectly in tune to the same rhythm.

But is this all to the relationship of the argonauta— this private pattern of two dancers perfectly in time? Should they not also be in tune with a larger rhythm, a natural swinging of the pendulum between sharing and solitude; between the intimate and the abstract; between the particular and the universal, the near and the far? And is it not the swinging of the pendulum between these opposite poles that makes a relationship nourishing? Yeats once said that the supreme experience of life was "to share profound thought and then to touch." But it takes both.

First touch, intimate touch of the personal and particular (the chores in the kitchen, the talk by the fire); then the loss of intimacy in the great stream of the impersonal and abstract (the silent beach, the

bowl of stars overhead). Both partners are lost in a
common sea of the universal which absorbs and yet
frees, which separates and yet unites. Is this not what
the more mature relationship, the meeting of two
solitudes, is meant to be? The double-sunrise stage
was only intimate and personal. The oyster bed was
caught in the particular and the functional. But the
argonauta, should they not be able to swing from the
intimate and the particular and the functional out
into the abstract and the universal, and then back to
the personal again?

And in this image of the pendulum swinging in
easy rhythm between opposite poles, is there not a
clue to the problem of relationships as a whole? Is
there not here even a hint of an understanding and
an acceptance of the wingèd life of relationships, of
their eternal ebb and flow, of their inevitable intermittency? "The life of the spirit," said Saint-Exupéry,
"the veritable life, is intermittent and only the life
of the mind is constant. . . . The spirit . . . alternates
between total vision and absolute blindness. Here is a
man, for example, who loves his farm—but there are

moments when he sees in it only a collection of unrelated objects. Here is a man who loves his wife—but there are moments when he sees in love nothing but burdens, hindrances, constraints. Here is a man who loves music—but there are moments when it cannot reach him."

The "veritable life" of our emotions and our relationships also is intermittent. When you love someone you do not love them all the time, in exactly the same way, from moment to moment. It is an impossibility. It is even a lie to pretend to. And yet this is exactly what most of us demand. We have so little faith in the ebb and flow of life, of love, of relationships. We leap at the flow of the tide and resist in terror its ebb. We are afraid it will never return. We insist on permanency, on duration, on continuity; when the only continuity possible, in life as in love, is in growth, in fluidity—in freedom, in the sense that the dancers are free, barely touching as they pass, but partners in the same pattern. The only real security is not in owning or possessing, not in demanding or expecting, not in hoping, even. Security in a relationship lies neither in looking back to what it was in nostalgia, nor forward to what it might be in dread or anticipation, but living in the present relationship and accepting it as it is now. For relationships too must be like islands. One must accept them for what they are here and now, within their limits—islands, surrounded and interrupted by the sea, continually visited and abandoned by the tides. One must accept the security of the wingèd life, of ebb and flow, of intermittency.

Intermittency—an impossible lesson for human beings to learn. How can one learn to live through the ebb-tides of one's existence? How can one learn to take the trough of the wave? It is easier to understand here on the beach, where the breathlessly still ebb tides reveal another life below the level which mortals usually reach. In this crystalline moment of suspense, one has a sudden revelation of the secret kingdom at the bottom of the sea. Here in the shallow flats one finds, wading through warm ripples, great horse conchs pivoting on a leg; white sand dollars, marble medallions engraved in the mud; and myriads of bright-colored cochina-clams, glistening in the foam, their shells opening and shutting like butterflies' wings. So beautiful is the still hour of the sea's withdrawal, as beautiful as the sea's return when the encroaching waves pound up the beach, pressing to reach those dark rumpled chains of seaweed which mark the last high tide.

Perhaps this is the most important thing for me to take back from beach-living: simply the memory that each cycle of the tide is valid; each cycle of the wave is valid; each cycle of a relationship is valid. And my shells? I can sweep them all into my pocket. They are only there to remind me that the sea recedes and returns eternally.

· 7 ·

A FEW SHELLS

I am packing to leave my island. What have I for my efforts, for my ruminations on the beach? What answers or solutions have I found for my life? I have a few shells in my pocket, a few clues, only a few.

When I think back to my first days here, I realize how greedily I collected. My pockets bulged with wet shells, the damp sand clinging to their crevices. The beach was covered with beautiful shells and I could not let one go by unnoticed. I couldn't even walk head up looking out to sea, for fear of missing something precious at my feet. The collector walks with blinders on; he sees nothing but the prize. In fact, the acquisitive instinct is incompatible with true appreciation of beauty. But after all the pockets were stretched and damp, and the bookcase shelves filled and the window ledges covered, I began to drop my acquisitiveness. I began to discard from my possessions, to select.

One cannot collect all the beautiful shells on the beach. One can collect only a few, and they are more beautiful if they are few. One moon shell is more impressive than three. There is only one moon in the sky. One double-sunrise is an event; six are a succession, like a week of school days. Gradually one discards and keeps just the perfect specimen; not necessarily a rare shell, but a perfect one of its kind. One sets it apart by itself, ringed around by space—like the island.

For it is only framed in space that beauty blooms. Only in space are events and objects and people

A Few Shells

unique and significant—and therefore beautiful. A tree has significance if one sees it against the empty face of sky. A note in music gains significance from the silences on either side. A candle flowers in the space of night. Even small and casual things take on significance if they are washed in space, like a few autumn grasses in one corner of an Oriental painting, the rest of the page bare.

My life in Connecticut, I begin to realize, lacks this quality of significance and therefore of beauty, because there is so little empty space. The space is scribbled on; the time has been filled. There are so few empty pages in my engagement pad, or empty hours in the day, or empty rooms in my life in which to stand alone and find myself. Too many activities, and people, and things. Too many worthy activities, valuable things and interesting people. For it is not merely the trivial which clutters our lives but the important as well. We can have a surfeit of treasures—an excess of shells, where one or two would be significant.

Here on this island I have had space. Paradoxically, in this limited area, space has been forced upon me. The geographical boundaries, the physical limitations, the restrictions on communication, have enforced a natural selectivity. There are not too many activities or things or people, and each one, I find, is significant, set apart in the frame of sufficient time and space. Here there is time; time to be quiet; time to work without pressure; time to think; time to watch the heron, watching with frozen patience for his prey. Time to look at the stars or to study a shell; time to see friends, to gossip, to laugh, to talk. Time, even, *not* to talk. At home, when I meet my friends in those cubby-holed hours, time is so precious we feel we must cram every available instant with conversation. We cannot afford the luxury of silence. Here on the island I find I can sit with a friend without talking, sharing the day's last sliver of pale green light on the horizon, or the whorls in a small white shell, or the dark scar left in a dazzling night sky by a shooting star. Then communication becomes communion and one is nourished as one never is by words.

Island living selects for me, but it is a natural, not an artificial selection. It selects numerically but not

A Few Shells

in kind. There are all kinds of experiences on this island, but not too many. There are all kinds of people, but not too many. The simplicity of life forces me into physical as well as intellectual or social activity. I have no car, so I bicycle for my supplies and my mail. When it is cold, I collect driftwood for my fireplace and chop it up too. I swim instead of taking hot baths. I bury my garbage instead of having it removed by a truck. And when I cannot write a poem, I bake biscuits and feel just as pleased. Most of these physical chores would be burdens at home, where my life is crowded and schedules are tight. There I have a house full of children and I am responsible for many people's lives. Here, where there is time and space, the physical tasks are a welcome change. They balance my life in a way I find refreshing and in which I seldom feel refreshed at home. Making beds or driving to market is not as refreshing as swimming or bicycling or digging in the earth. I cannot go on burying the garbage when I get home, but I can dig in a garden; I can bicycle to the cabin where I work; and I can remember to bake biscuits on bad days.

Gift from the Sea

My island selects for me socially too. Its small circumference cannot hold too many people. I see people here that I would not see at home, people who are removed from me by age or occupation. In the suburbs of a large city we tend to see people of the same general age and interests. That is why we chose the suburbs, because we have similar needs and pursuits. My island selects for me people who are very different from me—the stranger who turns out to be, in the frame of sufficient time and space, invariably interesting and enriching. I discover here what everyone has experienced on an ocean voyage or a long train ride or a temporary seclusion in a small village. Out of the welter of life, a few people are selected for us by the accident of temporary confinement in the same circle. We never would have chosen these neighbors; life chose them for us. But thrown together on this island of living, we stretch to understand each other and are invigorated by the stretching. The difficulty with big city environment is that if we select—and we must in order to live and breathe and work in such crowded conditions—we tend to select people like ourselves, a

A Few Shells

very monotonous diet. All hors d'oeuvres and no meat; or all sweets and no vegetables, depending on the kind of people we are. But however much the diet may differ between us, one thing is fairly certain: we usually select the known, seldom the strange. We tend not to choose the unknown which might be a shock or a disappointment or simply a little difficult to cope with. And yet it is the unknown with all its disappointments and surprises that is the most enriching.

In so many ways this island selects for me better than I do myself at home. When I go back will I be submerged again, not only by centrifugal activities, but by too many centripetal ones? Not only by distractions but by too many opportunities? Not only by dull people but by too many interesting ones? The multiplicity of the world will crowd in on me again with its false sense of values. Values weighed in quantity, not quality; in speed, not stillness; in noise, not silence; in words, not in thoughts; in acquisitiveness, not beauty. How shall I resist the onslaught? How shall I remain whole against the strains and stresses of "Zerrissenheit"?

Gift from the Sea

For the natural selectivity of the island I will have to substitute a conscious selectivity based on another sense of values—a sense of values I have become more aware of here. Island-precepts, I might call them if I could define them, signposts toward another way of living. Simplicity of living, as much as possible, to retain a true awareness of life. Balance of physical, intellectual and spiritual life. Work without pressure. Space for significance and beauty. Time for solitude and sharing. Closeness to nature to strengthen understanding and faith in the intermittency of life: life of the spirit, creative life and the life of human relationships. A few shells.

Island living has been a lens through which to examine my own life in the North. I must keep my lens when I go back. Little by little one's holiday vision tends to fade. I must remember to see with island eyes. The shells will remind me; they must be my island eyes.

· 8 ·

THE BEACH AT
MY BACK

I pick up my sisal bag. The sand slips softly under my feet. The time for reflection is almost over.

The search for outward simplicity, for inner integrity, for fuller relationship—is this not a limited outlook? Of course it is, in one sense. Today a kind of planetal point of view has burst upon mankind. The world is rumbling and erupting in ever-widening circles around us. The tensions, conflicts and sufferings even in the outermost circle touch us all, reverberate in all of us. We cannot avoid these vibrations.

But just how far can we implement this planetal awareness? We are asked today to feel compassionately for everyone in the world; to digest intellectually all the information spread out in public print; and to implement in action every ethical impulse aroused by our hearts and minds. The interrelatedness of the world links us constantly with more people than our hearts can hold. Or rather—for I believe the heart is infinite—modern communication loads us with more problems than the human frame can carry. It is good, I think, for our hearts, our minds, our imaginations to be stretched; but body, nerve, endurance and life-span are not as elastic. My life cannot implement in action the demands of all the people to whom my heart responds. I cannot marry all of them, or bear them all as children, or care for them all as I would my parents in illness or old age. Our grandmothers, and even—with some scrambling—our mothers, lived in a circle small enough to let them implement in action most of the impulses of their hearts and minds. We were brought up in a tradition that has now become impossible, for we have extended our circle through-out space and time.

Faced with this dilemma what can we do? How can we adjust our planetal awareness to our Puritan conscience? We are forced to make some compro-mise. Because we cannot deal with the many as indi-viduals, we sometimes try to simplify the many into an abstraction called the mass. Because we cannot deal with the complexity of the present, we often over-ride it and live in a simplified dream of the future. Because we cannot solve our own problems right here at home, we talk about problems out there in the world. An escape process goes on from the intolerable burden we have placed upon ourselves. But can one really feel deeply for an abstraction called the mass? Can one make the future a substitute for the present? And what guarantee have we that the future will be any better if we neglect the present? Can one solve world problems when one is unable to solve one's own? Where have we arrived in this process? Have we been successful, working at the periphery of the circle and not at the center?

If we stop to think about it, are not the real casualties in modern life just these centers I have been discussing: the here, the now, the individual and his relationships? The present is passed over in the race for the future; the here is neglected in favor of the there; and the individual is dwarfed by the enormity of the mass. America, which has the most glorious present still existing in the world today, hardly stops to enjoy it, in her insatiable appetite for the future. Perhaps the historian or the sociologist or the philosopher would say that we are still propelled by our frontier energy, still conditioned by our pioneer pressures or our Puritan anxiety to "do ye next thing." Europe, on the other hand, which we think of as being enamored of the past, has since the last war, strangely enough, been forced into a new appreciation of the present. The good past is so far away and the near past is so horrible and the future is so perilous, that the present has a chance to expand into a golden eternity of here and now. Europeans today are enjoying the moment even if it means merely a walk in the country on Sunday or sipping a cup of black coffee at a sidewalk café.

Perhaps we never appreciate the here and now

until it is challenged, as it is beginning to be today even in America. And have we not also been awakened to a new sense of the dignity of the individual because of the threats and temptations to him, in our time, to surrender his individuality to the mass— whether it be industry or war or standardization of thought and action? We are now ready for a true appreciation of the value of the here and the now and the individual.

The here, the now and the individual have always been the special concern of the saint, the artist, the poet and—from time immemorial—the woman. In the small circle of the home she has never quite forgotten the particular uniqueness of each member of the family; the spontaneity of now; the vividness of here. This is the basic substance of life. These are the individual elements that form the bigger entities like mass, future, world. We may neglect these elements, but we cannot dispense with them. They are the drops that make up the stream. They are the essence of life itself. It may be our special function to emphasize again these neglected realities, not as a retreat from greater responsibilities but as a first real step toward a deeper understanding and solution of them. When we start at the center of ourselves, we discover something worthwhile extending toward the periphery of the circle. We find again some of the joy in the now, some of the peace in the here, some of the love in me and thee which go to make up the kingdom of heaven on earth.

The waves echo behind me. Patience—Faith—Openness, is what the sea has to teach. Simplicity—Solitude—Intermittency...But there are other beaches to explore. There are more shells to find. This is only a beginning.

GIFT FROM THE SEA
RE-OPENED

Looking back at a book published twenty years ago, written in the midst of a busy family life, my chief sensation is astonishment. The original astonishment remains, never quite dimmed over the years, that a book of essays, written to work out my own problems, should have spoken to so many other women. Next comes an embarrassed astonishment at re-reading my naïve assumption in the book that the "victories" ("liberation" is the current word, but I spoke of "victories") in women's coming of age had been largely won by the Feminists of my mother's generation. I realize in hindsight and humility how great and how many were—and are—the victories still to be won. And finally a new development puzzles me: that after so many years, and such great achievement by women, my book should continue to be read.

Why should *Gift from the Sea*, after all we have undergone in these tumultuous twenty years, have any validity for a new generation of women? To look back on those years is a sobering experience. We have lived through the terms of four presidents and the assassination of one. We have wrestled with the tragedy of a long, divisive and conscience-searing war. We have witnessed shattering advances in science and technology. We have watched a man walk on the moon. We have been rocked by political and economic tremors that are still in force and worldwide. All of us have been swept forward by the ground swells of revolutionary social movements, most of them still in progress and not wholly defined by their popular labels. Among those the most important seem to me to be the Civil Rights movement, the so-called Counterculture, Women's Liberation and the Environmental Crisis. (It is interesting to note that woman has taken as influential a role in the three movements which do not bear her name as in the movement she calls her own.)

The world has totally changed in twenty years and so, of course, have the lives of every one of us, including my own. When I wrote *Gift from the Sea,* I was still in the stage of life I called "the oyster bed," symbol of a spreading family and growing children. The oyster bed, as the tide of life ebbed and the children went away to school, college, marriage or careers, was left high and dry. A most uncomfortable stage followed, not sufficiently anticipated and barely hinted at in my book. In bleak honesty it can only be called "the abandoned shell." Plenty of solitude, and a sudden panic at how to fill it, characterize this period. With me, it was not a question of simply filling up the space or the time. I had many activities and even a wellestablished vocation to pursue. But when a mother is left, the lone hub of a wheel, with no other lives revolving about her, she faces a total re-orientation. It takes time to re-find the center of gravity.

All the inner and outer exploration a woman has done earlier in life pays off when she reaches the abandoned shell. One has to come to terms with oneself not only in a new stage of life but in a new role. Life without children, living for oneself—the words at first ring with a hollow sound.

But with effort, patience and a sympathetic and supportive husband, one wins through to the adventure of an "Argonauta." My husband and I even named our last home, on the island of Maui, "Argonauta." For me, because of my husband's death, the Argonauta stage was sadly of very brief duration. I am again faced with woman's recurring lesson. To quote my own words, "woman must come of age by herself—she must find her true center alone." The lesson seems to need re-learning about every twenty years in a woman's life.

What then has a grandmother and a widow to give the new generation of women in the oyster bed?

Gift from the Sea Re-opened

Admiration, first of all. As I look at my daughters, my daughters-in-law, my nieces and my young friends, I am astounded at what they accomplish. They are better mothers than I was and they are the admitted equals of their husbands in intelligence and initiative. They have no domestic "help" in their homes and yet with vigilant planning, some skillful acrobatics and far more help from their husbands than any previous generation, they manage to lead enriching lives, including special interests of their own. They go out to work or they study; they write or they teach; they weave or paint or play in musical groups; they are often involved in civic activities. Sometimes they do several of those things at once.

Are they happy—or shall I say, happier than my generation? This is a question I cannot answer. In a sense, I think it irrelevant. Without hesitation I can affirm that they are more honest, more courageous in facing themselves and their lives, more confident of what they want to do and more efficient in carrying through their aims. But, above all, they are more aware.

Gift from the Sea

Perhaps the greatest progress, humanly speaking, in these past twenty years, for both women and men, is in the growth of consciousness. In fact, those movements I mentioned under their popular labels could be more truly described as enlargements in consciousness. A new consciousness of the dignity and rights of an individual, regardless of race, creed, class or sex. A new consciousness and questioning of the materialistic values of the Western world. A new consciousness of our place in the universe, and a new awareness of the inter-relatedness of all life on our planet.

For women, much of this new awareness is due to the Women's Liberation movement. Enlightenment has filtered down to a vast audience through the public media. Talks, programs, courses and articles have been addressed to women and concerned with their lives. New ground has been opened up, revealing the undiscovered depths of woman's emotional life, through the pioneering literature of brilliant writers such as Florida Scott Maxwell, Anaïs Nin, Simone de Beauvoir, Doris Lessing and, in our own

country, writers as diverse as Elizabeth Janeway a
May Sarton. The best "growing ground" for wome
however, may be in the widespread mushroomin
of women's discussion groups of all types and sizes
Women are talking to each other, not simply in private in the kitchen, in the nursery or over the back
fence, as they have done through the ages, but in
public groups. They are airing their problems, dis-
covering themselves and comparing their experiences. More important, they are beginning to talk to
men, openly and honestly, often arguing and chal-
lenging, but at last trying to explain what they felt
could never be explained. They retreat less often
behind that age-old screen of women: "If you don't
understand, I can't possibly tell you." (How arrogant
to assume your partner cannot understand!) And
men, to their great credit, for the most part are listening and, I believe, understanding more than we
ever expected.

Much of this exploration and new awareness is
uncomfortable and painful for both men and women.
Growth in awareness has always been painful. (One

Gift from the Sea

ed only remember one's own adolescence or watch
e's adolescent children.) But it does lead to greater
dependence and, eventually, cooperation in action.
or the enormous problems that face the world today,
in both the private and the public sphere, cannot be
solved by women—or by men—alone. They can only
be surmounted by men and women side by side.

1975

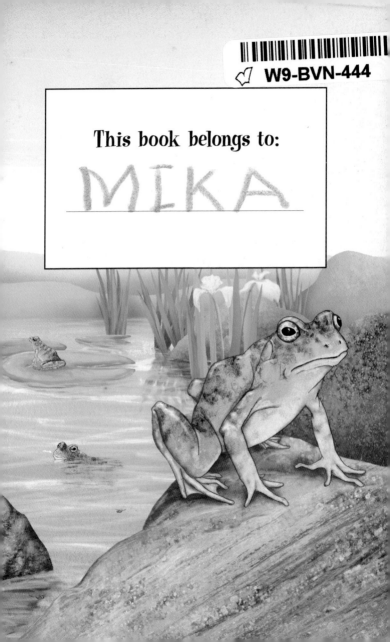

This book belongs to:

MIKA

Published by Ladybird Books Ltd
A Penguin Company
Penguin Books Ltd, 80 Strand, London WC2R 0RL, UK
Penguin Books Australia Ltd, Camberwell, Victoria, Australia
Penguin Books (NZ) Ltd, Cnr Airbourne and Rosedale Roads, Albany, Auckland, 1310, New Zealand

1 3 5 7 9 10 8 6 4 2

Printed in Italy

Tadpoles and Frogs

written by Lorraine Horsley
illustrated by Sharon Harmer

Frogs can live in water
and on land.

This frog lays her eggs
in the water.

eggs

The Marsupial Frog carries her eggs and tadpoles on her back.

A little tadpole comes out
of an egg.
It has gills to help it to
breathe in the water like
a fish.

egg

tadpole

gills

After a few weeks, the tadpole will grow lungs.

The little tadpole gets bigger and bigger.
It has teeth to help it to eat plants in the water.

plant

tadpole

After a few weeks, the tadpole
will start to eat insects.

The little tadpole gets
bigger and bigger.
It has a long tail to help
it to swim in the water.

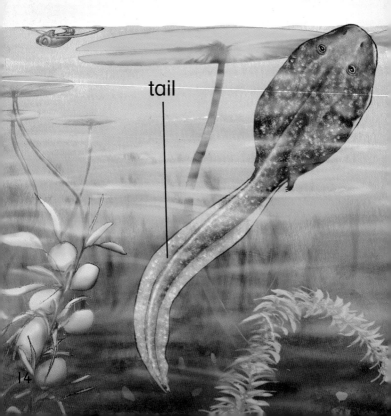

tail

s-shape

The tadpole swims by making
s-shapes with its long tail.

The tadpole grows two back legs.
The legs have webbed toes to help the tadpole to swim fast.

back legs

webbed toes

The African Bullfrog
has short toes
to help it to
burrow under
the ground.

The tadpole grows two
front legs.
The tadpole's tail gets
smaller and smaller.

tail

front legs

The Red-eyed
Treefrog has
sticky toes to
help it hold on
to leaves and
branches.

The tadpole is now a
little frog.
It comes out of the water.

little frog

A frog can see above, below, in front and behind with its big eyes.

21

The frog has a long
sticky tongue to help
it to catch flies to eat.

fly

tongue

Frogs close their eyes to help push down their food to swallow.

The frog has long legs
to help it to jump.

long legs

The African Running
Frog does not jump!
It walks or runs
because the
grass is
too tall.

The frog has to look for
a mate.
She hears a male frog
calling.

male frog

ear

The African Reed
Frog can puff
up its throat
to make very
loud calls.

27

The frog lays her eggs
in the water.

Do you know what
happens next?

Glossary

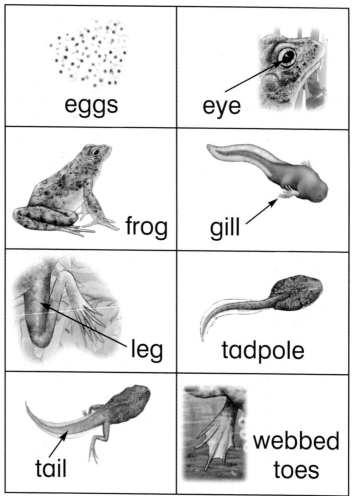

eggs	eye
frog	gill
leg	tadpole
tail	webbed toes